THE BATTLE OF TOURS

The Turning Point in the Struggle Against Islam

Written by Xavier De Weirt
In collaboration with Mathieu Beaud
Translated by Carly Probert

History | 50MINUTES.com

THE BATTLE OF TOURS

KEY INFORMATION

- **When:** 25 October 732
- **Where:** At Moussais (later renamed *Moussais-la-Bataille*), a municipality of Vouneuil-sur-Vienne between Poitiers and Châtellerault (France)
- **Context:** The Muslim expansion in the West and the fight for power in the Frankish area
- **Belligerents:** The Frankish kingdom and the Duchy of Aquitaine against the Umayyad Caliphate of Damascus
- **Commanders and leaders:**
  - Charles, later nicknamed Charles Martel, a Frankish prince (c. 684-741)
  - Odo the Great, duke of Aquitaine (mid-7th century-735)
  - Abdul Rahman Al Ghafiqi, governor of Cordoba (died 732)
- **Outcome:** Frankish victory
- **Victims:**
  - Frankish and Aquitaine camp: approximately 1 000 deaths
  - Umayyad camp: approximately 12 000 deaths

INTRODUCTION

The Battle of Tours – also known as the Battle of Poitiers – was fought on 25 October 732, a few kilometers from the Poitiers capital, between the Franks led by the mayor of the Austrasian palace, Charles (the future Charles Martel), who had come to assist the Duke Odo of Aquitaine, and the

Arab-Berber troops led by the governor of Cordoba, Abdul Rahman Al Ghafiqi.

Although it is impossible today, due to lack of specific sources, to say with certainty when and where the battle took place and what the forces were, it has long been held that the victory of the Franks marked a definitive end to the Muslim expansion in the West. However, it has already been made clear that the Battle of Tours was, in reality, more of a defensive response to a raid orchestrated by the Arab troops targeting the shrine of St. Martin of Tours than a real initiative to bring a definitive end to the attempted conquest of Gaul by the Umayyads (dynasty of caliphs who ruled between 660 and 750 from Damascus, over an empire established around the Mediterranean basin).

POLITICAL AND SOCIAL CONTEXT

Above all, it is useful to clarify the limitations of the topic: unlike more recent conflicts, there are relatively few sources that discuss the Battle of Tours. Archaeology does not offer any assistance here and literary sources should be subject to scrutiny to avoid the pitfall of taking the information provided by the often biased columnists at face value. Moreover, contemporary sources or those following the event provide little information on the subject. Some Latin chronicles that have no particular interest in tackling the topic – such as that of Venerable Bede (Anglo-Saxon Benedictine monk and doctor of the Church, 672-735), *An Ecclesiastical History of the English People* (735), or the *Continuation of the Chronicle of Fredegar* (written around 736), or the *Chronicle of Moissac* (compiled in the early 9th century) – paint the progress of the Arab troops in Gaul, the looting they perpetrated, or the "punishment" inflicted on the Arabs in Poitiers in broad strokes. The best description – if any – can be found in a Mozarabic chronicle (Latin chronicle composed by a Christian writer from Cordoba, c. 754) entitled *Epitoma Imperatorum*. On the Arab side, few contemporary sources or sources immediately following the battle mention the episode. However, we can mention *The Conquest of Egypt, North Africa and Spain* from Egyptian historian Ibn 'Abd al-Hakam (mid-9th century). Other historians were silent on the subject of this battle. It is therefore particularly difficult to estimate the number of soldiers who took part in the battle and most of the data available is extremely controversial. Nonetheless, we can propose, with all the necessary caution, the figures of 15 000 to 20 000 men on the

Franks and Aquitanian side (including 1 000 casualties) and 20 000-25 000 for the Umayyad troops (including 12 000 casualties, among which was Abdul Rahman Al Ghafiqi).

Battle of Tours, October 732 by Charles de Steuben, between 1834 and 1837.

THE UMAYYAD CALIPHATE IN THE CONQUEST OF THE WEST

A power from elsewhere

Governed from Damascus, the Umayyad Caliphate repre-sented, in the early 8th century, a vast empire stretching from the borders of India to the Atlantic. From the late 7th century, it conquered much of the eastern territories of the Byzantine Empire, attacked Constantinople (formerly Byzantium and modern-day Istanbul) and definitively took over North Africa with the capture of Carthage in 702, after a conquest that lasted several decades. Arriving in Europe, in modern-day Gibraltar, the caliph's troops seized almost all of the Iberian Peninsula fighting the Visigoths (people of German origin), who were less combative and divided. Indeed, the Visigoth monarchy had been decaying for the last century and had been increasingly weakened by riots and conspiracies. The conquest of the peninsula began in the spring of 711, with several raids of recognition. Notably, the Visigoth King Roderic (died in 711) was defeated on the River Guadelate, near Cadiz, after facing the 7 000 Berbers (population of North and Saharan Africa), led by Tarik ibn Ziyad (Berber leader, 8th century), in the service of Musa ibn Nusayr (640-718), then governor of North Africa, on behalf of the caliph of Damascus. This battle marked the defeat of the Visigoth monarchy, culminating in the death of Roderic on the battlefield and decimating the nobility. Quickly, their positions gave way one after the other in the face of the Umayyad advance: Cordoba, Seville, Toledo (capital of the Visigoth kingdom), Zaragoza, etc.

Visigoth King Roderic during the Battle of Gadelate, by Bernardo Blanco y Pérez, 1871.

GOOD TO KNOW

The dynasty of the Umayyad caliphs governed the conquered empire around the Mediterranean between 660 and 750. Their capital was Damascus. The Battle of Tours took place during the reign of Caliph Hisham Abu al-Walid (691-743), the reign of whom was marked by the military apogee of the caliphate.

To consolidate their grip on these new lands, the Arabs negotiated and imposed the payment of heavy tributes. It only took the governors between three and five years to complete the conquest of al-Andalus and to Islamize the country on behalf of the caliph. However, conversions, the first of which took place during the reign of Walid I (died 715), were not systematic and populations continued to practice their religions (Judaism and Christianity) in exchange for payment of a tax (the *jizya*).

The loss of momentum of the conquest

Although, from 711 to 756, twenty governors acting on behalf of the Damascus Caliph succeeded to the head of al-Andalus, links with the capital were beginning to distend from 725. The distance from the central power, the rise of autonomies in the peninsula, the wealth distribution problems, local agreements and alliances with indigenous peoples and the Berber revolts caused many internal struggles that weakened the central power, affecting the momentum of the conquest northward and prohibiting any new offensive for the territorial expansion of al-Andalus.

Once settled in the peninsula, the Muslims set their eyes on the other side of the Pyrenees. The expansion was entering a new phase: indeed, it took the form of *gazawat* ("raids"), where the troops of the caliph penetrated into Gaul. They first attacked the Septimania, a Visigoth territory (which corresponds to the Mediterranean Languedoc and Roussillon). Many places were then subject to incursions: Narbonne fell in 719, Carcassonne in 725. However, not all the Arab attempts were successful. In 721, Duke Odo of Aquitaine managed to break the siege of Toulouse and repel the attacks of the *Wali* ("governor") Al-Samh ibn Malik al-Khawlani (died 721). At the same time, in the East, the Arab troops encountered new difficulties facing the Byzantine

Empire and failed in Constantinople (718).

In early 730, the movement of conquest was running out of steam for several reasons:

- Firstly, the surprise effect had worn off;
- A number of fighters – including the Berbers who travelled with their families – now wanted to settle down and enjoy the rewards of their conquest, while the distance from major centers of the Caliphate and the capital in particular complicated the stewardship of such an empire;
- Having finally reached the edge of the regions where climate conditions were similar to their home countries, the Arab troops now faced a hostile climate where cold and humidity mingled, to which they were not accustomed.

THE RISE TO POWER OF THE PIPPINID DYNASTY AND THE ESTABLISHMENT OF THE CAROLINGIAN SYSTEM

Taking advantage of the fall of the Roman Empire in 476, Childeric I (458-481/482), the Germanic leader at the head of the Salian Franks, established a kingdom from the Scheldt valley to the valley of the Somme. His son Clovis (465-511) extended his kingdom at the expense of the Romans to the south and east (in particular, winning the so-called victory of Soissons in 486), the Alemanni (Germanic people) who were pushed back beyond the Rhine in 505, the Visigoths (with the victory of Vouillé, near Poitiers in 506/507) and the Ripaurian Franks (510). Clovis' baptism by Bishop Remi (estimated date between 498 and 508) made the Frankish kingdom the first Catholic barbarian kingdom. In turn, his son conquered the kingdom of the Burgunds (people of Scandinavian origin) in 534 and Provence in 537. However, the stability and power of the Frankish kingdom were threatened by succession issues (first with the death of Clovis in 511, then the death of Chlothar I in 561). Indeed, despite the maintaining of a single royal power in theory, each king's son claimed part of the kingdom. The divisions and wars were linked, causing the individualization of three kingdoms: Neustria (between the Seine and Loire), Austrasia (northeast) and Burgundy (southeast). Aquitaine, as part of the Frankish kingdom, was in turn divided into three. Having become a difficult area to control, it rapidly gained autonomy. Further afield, other peoples such as the Frisians in Lower Rhine or the Vasques in the southwest of Gaul threatened the borders of the Frankish kingdom. Between 570 and 613, the Neustrians and Austrasians cla-shed violently in a *faide* (a private revenge), promoting the rise of the aristocracy who chose the mayor of the palace in the different realms. Among these aristocratic families on the rise, that of Pepin of Landen (c. 580-640) – also known as Pepin the Elder – who, from 613, became mayor of the palace of Austrasia, stood out.

Good to know

Under the Merovingians, the term "mayor" means "administrator of royal estates, responsible for the 'domestics' of the palace and its movements, as well as governor of all its members, responsible for the

Treasury and the army" (Touati 2000, p. 190). Becoming the equivalent of a Prime Minister, his power continued to increase to the point of allowing Pepin the Short (715-768), son of Charles Martel, to officially take the place of the king in 751.

Succession crisis and rivalries in the palace

Pepin the Younger, king of France, engraving from *Chroniques des ducs de Brabant* by Adrian de Barlande, published in 1603.

In 687, Pepin, the grandson of Pepin the Elder, Pepin of Herstal (645-714) – also known as Pepin the Younger – Mayor of the Palace of Austrasia from 679, triumphed over the mayor of the palace of Neustrasia at the Battle of Tertry. He then took the title of *princeps Francorum* ("Prince of the Franks"). However, he did not cast aside the Merovingian king, who retained his title despite his non-existent power. From then on, Pepin of Herstal tried to restore the ancient boundaries of the Merovingian kingdom: south of Loire, his authority was zero, just as in Burgundy. When he died on 16 December 714, a succession crisis broke out: it was his grandson Theodoald, son of the mayor of the palace of Neustrasia Grimoald, aged just six, who was expected to succeed him, under the regency of his grandmother Plectrude (7th-8th century), the first wife of Pepin of Herstal. For fear of being excluded from power, she immediately had Charles incarcerated to prevent him from claiming the title and ousting Theodoald. Charles was another of Pepin of Hertsal's sons, though illegitimate. However, the presence of a woman and a child in power opened a breach, which all the powerful people of the kingdom who wanted to free themselves of the strong influence exercised by the mayor of the palace beforehand rushed to infiltrate. A revolt broke out: the nobles of Neustria made Ragenfred (died 731) mayor of the palace and drove away those who were faithful to the regent. In 715, the death of the Merovingian King Dagobert II (699-715) allowed the Neustrian nobility to stage another coup: indeed, the late king had left only one son, Thierry (died 737), who was still a child and whom they managed to oust. In his place, they imposed a clerk named Daniel (son of Childeric II), who was crowned under the name of Chilperic II

(670-721). Making alliances with the Frisians and the Saxons, victims of the "Austrasian steamroller" (Lebecq 1990, p. 192), Ragenfred launched several successful expeditions against the Austrasians and against Plectrude, who ended up giving him the Treasury of the Neustro-Burgundian kingdom in 716.

At the same time, the confusion generated as a result allowed Charles to escape from prison. He rallied the vanquished Austrasians to his cause and obtained two victories over Ragenfred and his men: the first was in 716, at the Ambleve (near Malmedy) and the second was in 717 in Vinchy (near Cambrai). Strengthened by this success, Charles led several punitive expeditions from 719 against the northern people allied with the Neastrians. After chasing the Saxons, he began the reconquest of the part of Friesland his father had captured. Meanwhile, Ragenfred allied with Odo, the Duke of Aquitaine, whose troops had already crossed the Loire and rallied the Neustrian armies near Paris. Between Senlis and Soissons, in Nery, on 14 October 719, Charles sent his two opponents running: Ragenfred fled to Angers, where he established a strong principality that would stand up to the authority of Charles until 731, while Odo re-crossed the Loire, taking Chilperic II with him, as well as the very rich treasure made up of precious fabrics and silverware. Around 720-721, Charles offered Odo the Great peace in exchange for the king and the spoils of war. For his part, Charles agreed to recognize the title of *princeps Aquitaniae* ("Prince of Aquitaine") and, in order to ensure the support of the Neustrians, he even recognized Chilperic II as *rex Francorum* ("king of the Franks"). On the latter's death in 723, it was the fallen son of Dagobert III, Thierry – now Thierry IV – who Charles placed on the throne, thereby ensuring his hands were free. From then on, in Neustria a puppet king sat on the throne, under the tutelage of an all-powerful Austrasian mayor of the palace.

Patronage and the defense of Christianity: the foundations of the Carolingian system

Faced with crumbling kingdoms, security was taken charge of by an emerging power: the aristocracy. To ensure their power, the nobles set up a system of protection granted to domestic warriors who tied themselves to them, in exchange for a recommendation. This new patronage revealed the beginnings of a social pattern – in this case, the vassalage – which would fully develop under the Carolingians (the dynasty succeeding the Merovingians) and on whose tight mesh Charles Martel relied to strengthen his position at the head of Austrasia.

In these times of general crisis, the Church also tried to deal with the different dangers that came both from within and from outside. The churchmen then mixed with politics, seeking to obtain privileges, and thus losing any real religious influence. Faced with the resurgence of paganism and the advance of Islam, given the politicization of the clergy, the answer to this problem was to be found in monasteries, the only entities that showed a true cultural and religious dynamism. By encouraging evangelical missions, Charles Martel offered protection to Boniface (whose real name was Wyndrid, born around 675 and martyred in 754), a monk of Anglo-Saxon origin, who was in charge of the evangelization of Germany and who, on the appointment of Pope Gregory III (died in 741), became bishop (742), then Bishop of Fulda (732). An essential intermediary in the establishment of new relationships between the papacy and the Frankish kings, Boniface became an ally of choice to defend Charles Martel as a "champion and defender" of Christianity in the face of the growing danger embodied by Islam. His goal was to federate the different peripheral peoples (those of Hesse, Thuringia and Bavaria in particular) around the Frankish kingdom through a sustained policy of Christianization. Evangelization became a "true public enterprise" (Rouche 1990, p. 50), making the new holder of the secular power the main ally of the spiritual power. This alliance was the second pillar on which the Carolingian dynasty would establish its authority over Europe.

St. Boniface Baptizing and Martyrdom in 754, illustration from the Fulda Sacramentary, fol. 126, 11th century.

The advance of Islam in Septimania therefore provided an ideal pretext for Charles Martel to intervene in Aquitaine. While one might think that Duke Odo of Aquitaine was at the height of his power after the victory gained over the troops of the Wali Al-Samh ibn Malik al-Khawlani in Toulouse in 721, he concluded, in order to prevent a new Muslim attack, an alliance with the Berber leader Munûsa, master of Cerdanya (the Eastern Pyrenees region), in rebellion against the new Wali Abd al-Rahman. Charles Martel took this opportunity to denounce the alliance of Aquitaine with the Infidels, and launched a campaign in 731 south of the Loire with a double aim: a rich tribute and, more importantly, the domination of the southwest territories which had escaped him until now. Thus, when Odo the Great begged him to fight at his side against the raids by Arab-Berber troops a year later, Charles Martel did not hesitate to accept.

COMMANDERS AND LEADERS

CHARLES MARTEL, MAYOR OF THE PALACE AND PRINCE OF THE FRANKS

Charles Martel, duc de Brabant, engraving from *Chroniques des ducs de Brabant* by Adrian de Barlande, published in 1603.

Son of the mayor of the palace, Pepin of Herstal, and his second wife, Alpaida, Charles managed to obtain the legacy of his father with the support of the Austrasian aristocracy against the Neustrians, Frisians and the Alemanni and Burgundians, and in turn became mayor of the palace. From 720-721, he asserted his power to the point where, on the death of the Merovingian King Thierry IV in 737, he did not appoint his successor. From the 9th century, the chroniclers nicknamed him Martellus ("hammer") to highlight the efficiency with which he was able to impose his power and rise to leader at the head of the Franks. In 732, his victory over the Arabs enabled him to establish Frankish supremacy over a rebellious Aquitaine. Strengthened by this success, he conquered Septimania and Provence in 736 and 739, thanks to Liutprand (died in 744), king of the Lombards. He died on 22 October 741 and was buried in Saint-Denis, beside the Merovingian kings.

ODO, DUKE OF AQUITAINE

When Odo rose to the head of Aquitaine, the Duchy extended from the Pyrenees to the Loire. Between 687 and 715, he managed to expand Aquitaine by taking possession of the Nivernais (territory almost corresponding to present-day Nievre), the Vivarais (Ardeche) and part of Provence, which he took from the Neustrian and Austrasian kings. He then formed an alliance with the nobles of Neustria to oppose Charles Martel, whose power continued to grow. However, the alliance did not last and, towards 720, Odo was forced to approach Charles Martel, with whom he concluded a peace treaty: he gave him Chilperic, King of

Neustria, and renounced his fight against Charles Martel. He triumphed over Al-Samh ibn Malik al-Khawlani in 721 at Toulouse, but he failed to contain all the movements of the Arab troops who took Nimes and Carcassonne four years later. In 731, he allied with the Berber leader, Munûsa, at the head of Cerdanya, to whom he gave his daughter's hand in marriage. However, Munûsa was killed during the punitive expedition against the fortress of al-Bab (likely Puycerda) in 731 by the men of Wali Abd al-Rahman al-Ghafiqi. When the Umayyads launched a new offensive in the north, they plundered Aquitaine and Bordeaux, obligating Odo the Great to seek help from Charles Martel. Following the Frankish victory at Poitiers, Odo recognized the authority of Charles Martel. He died in 735.

ABDUL RAHMAN AL GHAFIQI, GOVERNOR OF CORDOBA

Abdul Rahman Al Ghafiqi participated in the conquest of al-Andalus from 711. After the failure of the Arab-Berber troops against Toulouse in 721, he was chosen by the Wali of Cordoba to lead the troops beyond the Pyrenees. Becoming governor ten years later, he subdued the rebellion of Munûsa, the Berber leader who joined forces with the Duke of Aquitaine. He led his troops to victory in Bordeaux, but his ascent towards Tours was stopped by Charles Martel and his men. He died on the battlefield on 25 October 732.

ANALYSIS OF THE BATTLE

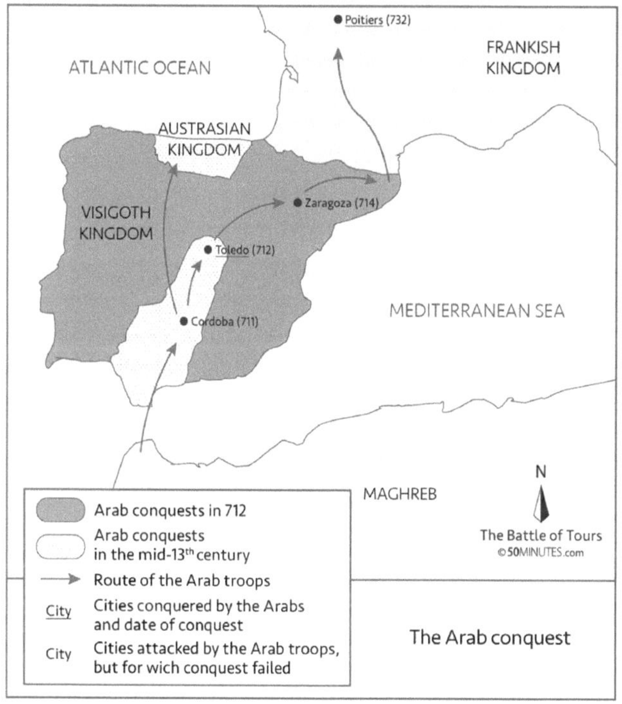

PREMISES OF THE BATTLE

Attacked in the south by the Umayyad troops, Aquitaine faced new challenges when the Arab-Berber troops passed the Pyrenees. In 721, the Wali Al-Samh ibn Malik al-Khawlani besieged Toulouse, but Odo the Great managed to repel the attack and kill the governor.

Note that while the Duke of Aquitaine feared attacks from the Pyrenees, the fact remained that he was still suspicious of Charles Martel, who still had his eyes set on his territory. In 731, he therefore made a covenant with a Berber chief, Munûsa, who strongly wished to be independent, to whom he gave his daughter's hand in marriage as a guarantee of this new pact. Rebellious, Munûsa refused to obey orders given by Abdul Rahman Al Ghafiqi to attack the Christians in the Southern Gaul, so that the governor's troops were released against him. He died during the fight in the stronghold of al-Bab. Decapitated, his head was sent to Damascus as a trophy, a symbol of the quelled rebellion, and his wife was sent to the harem of the caliph.

In 732, rather than attacking Toulouse, remembered as a place of defeat, the new governor Abdul Rahman Al Ghafiqi preferred to attack from the west, with Tours and the wealthy shrine of St. Martin as targets. He crushed Odo the Great near Bordeaux, plundered and devastated the outskirts of the city, then started his ascent towards Tours.

THE COURSE OF THE BATTLE

As mentioned above, few sources report precisely what happened in the Poitevin countryside on that autumn day in 732. Although historians now agree on the date, a large mystery remains: the forces present.

The *Chronicle of Moissac* compiled in 818 – the text of which builds on earlier documents for the period 717-776 – tells of the call for the holy way launched by the governor Abdul Rahman Al Ghafiqi in 731 in Pamplona (Navarre). Thus, nearly 20 000 men were brought together from the East and from Berber territory. Passing through Roncesvalles, they plundered Aquitaine unopposed, arrived in Bordeaux, seized Angouleme, Périgueux and Saintes. Now the Arab-Berber troops had only one goal: to reach the Loire to plunder St. Martin of Tours, grab its relics and rich treasure, made up of precious fabrics and silverware, brought by pilgrims. The Duke of Aquitaine, Odo, implored Charles Martel, "prince of the Franks" to rescue him. The *Chronicle* then mentions the "great army" that Charles Martel was able to gather, and the rout of the Saracens who "took flight and left Spain" (cited by Levillain and Samaran 1938, p. 245). Another text – commonly referred to as the *Continuation of the Chronicle of Fredegar*, compiled from 736 on the orders of Childebrand, the brother of Charles Martel, who participated in the event himself – relates the battle as follows:

> "The Saracens left their homes with their king named Abdirama, crossed the Garonne, reached Bordeaux; then, setting fire to churches, and killing people, they advanced to Poitiers; after burning the Basilica Saint-Hilaire, they decided to completely ruin that of St. Martin (Tours). Against them, the prince Charles boldly ranked his troops in battle" (*ibid:* 244).[1]

Thus, the two texts agree on the aim pursued by the troops of Abdul Rahman Al Ghafiqi: to reach the sanctuary of St. Martin of Tours. However, he was not counting on the inter-

---

1. This quotation has been translated by 50Minutes.com.

vention of Charles Martel and his men in the countryside of Poitiers. After a week of skirmishes, the final confrontation took place on 25 October 732: Abdul Rahman Al Ghafiqi launched his troops on horseback on the men of Charles Martel, but his men faced a true human rampart made up of the Franks, their swords in hand, in the case of the richest soldiers, and spears pointed at the enemy. It was thanks to the "strength of a well-organized defensive formation" (Guichard 2011) that the Franks were victorious. The Arab-Berber troops then attempted to retreat and were attacked from behind by the soldiers of the Duke of Aquitaine. Abdul Rahman Al Ghafiqi fell and died on the battlefield. On 26 October, while they were about to engage in battle once again, the Franks discovered the empty tents of the Arab camp: their enemies, probably clueless without their leader, fled, their only goal being to return to their lands.

REPERCUSSIONS OF THE BATTLE

IMMEDIATE CONSEQUENCES

As we can see, the Battle of Tours took place, on the one hand, in the context of an Umayyad conquest losing momentum and, on the other, during a process of strengthening of the Frankish power. Although from a historical point of view its importance has been exaggerated for a long time, it should be stressed that the confrontation of 732 represented a serious setback for the troops from Spain, just as it marked an important step towards the affirmation of the Pippinid dynasty – the future Carolingians. This certainly put a stop to Muslim incursions in Gaul, but it by no means put a definitive end to the Muslim presence north of the Pyrenees, since the Umayyad troops retained Narbonne until 759 and incursions continued to happen for nearly a century.

Until then, the troops of the Umayyad caliphate had truly met little resistance in their progression. Indeed, the conquest of the Iberian Peninsula was made without difficulties and the first incursions in Gaul were mostly successful. However, the rise – or rather, the recovery – of the new states, including that of the Franks under the authority of Charles Martel, changed the situation, causing real difficulties that the caliphate was not able to solve. Previously more interested in looting than settling, it was by renouncing to settle beyond the Pyrenees – in the wake of the Battle of Tours in 732 – that the issues of settlement and organization had to be considered by the rulers of the peninsula. The remoteness of the central governments and the revolts rising throughout the caliphate from the year 720 would cause the fall of the Umayyads in 750 and the rise of a new independent Iberian emirate around Cordoba.

On the side of the Franks, the Battle of Tours allowed Charles Martel to restore Frankish authority throughout the weakening Merovingian kingdom, to seize the coveted Aquitaine and to continue his policy of reconquest of the Merovingian kingdom: Burgundy and Lyon were defeated the following year, while Provence tried to resist by making an alliance with the Arabs, thus providing Charles Martel with an excuse to intervene in southern Gaul. However, beyond the territorial aspect, Charles Martel intended to rise to the head of the Christian world and, to do that, he wanted to establish himself as a fervent defender of Christ and his Church, claiming it was his mission to restore the preponderance of Christianity in the West. In a way, Tours therefore identified Charles Martel and his offspring as pro-tectors of the new faith, thus legitimizing the power they had usurped from the last Merovingians.

THE CONSTRUCTION OF A SYMBOL

"This battle does not possess the importance attributed to it [...] It marked the end of a raid, but did not truly stop any-thing. If Charles had been defeated, the result would have been only greater plunder."[2] (Pirenne, 2003). A decisive clash, or simply a "counter-raid", as said by Belgian historian Henri

---

2. This quotation has been translated from the original French edition of the book by 50Minutes.com.

Pirenne (1862-1935), the Battle of Tours caused ink to flow for centuries. Contemporary or immediately subsequent chroniclers attested to the imprint it left on the minds of the era: Charles Martel was described as a "brave warrior", acting "with the help of Christ" who "triumphed over the enemies"[3] (*Continuation of the Chronicle of Fredegar*: 244). Bede tells of the "punishment from God". Conversely, the medieval Arab chroniclers evoke the battle of Al-Shuhada Balat ("the alley of martyrs"). It was a religious ideological recuperation, but not only that, according to French historian Pierre Guichard (born 1939). Indeed, he notes the use of the term *Europenses* ("Europeans") by the anonymous chronicler of Cordoba to qualify the Franks, noting that the author – and probably his contemporaries – was "conscious (but to what extent?) of the 'geopolitical' issue of the conflict"[4] (Guichard, 2011).

It should also be stressed that the heroic figure of Charles Martel quickly gave way to that of his grandson, Charlemagne (King of the Franks and emperor, 742/747-814) and that the construction of the myth surrounding the Battle of Tours and its victor would only truly begin when the Muslim threat reappeared: firstly at the time of the Crusades (11th-13th century) and then when Constantinople fell to the Ottoman Empire in 1453. A vehicle of a nascent patriotism in the 19th century, the clash of Tours became a prime symbol, even to the point of exaggeration. Chateaubriand (French writer and politician, 1768-1848), echoing the words of Voltaire

---

3. This quotation has been translated by 50Minutes.com.
4. *Ibid.*

(French writer, 1694-1778) a few decades earlier, stigmatized the scope of the battle: "The Saracens had already crossed Spain, passed the Pyrenees, and flooded France to the Loire. Charles Martel crushed them between Tours and Poitiers, slaying more than three hundred thousand men (732). This was one of the greatest events in history: If the Sarrasiins had been victorious, the world would have been Mahommedan"[5] (Penaud and Penaud (eds.), 1831: 14). It was also in the 19th century that the episode was recovered and presented – and taught in public schools – as one of the first stages of the construction of the nation.

Even today, the historical debate becomes animated around the symbol and the still thriving imagination embodied by the Battle of Tours. However, one must conclude by repeating the words of renowned medievalists Philippe Senac and Françoise Michaud: "Many voices have been raised in trying to put the Battle of Tours in its right place. These efforts have been in vain, as, transformed into a symbol, the event has gone down in history along with its hero, Charles Martel. It belongs to this common ideological basis that became a foundation for the French nation, the Christian civilization, and the European identity in the staging of the clash of civilizations and the exclusion of the other"[6] (*Histoire de l'islam et des musulmans en France,* 2006: 15).

---

5. *Ibid.*
6. *Ibid.*

SUMMARY

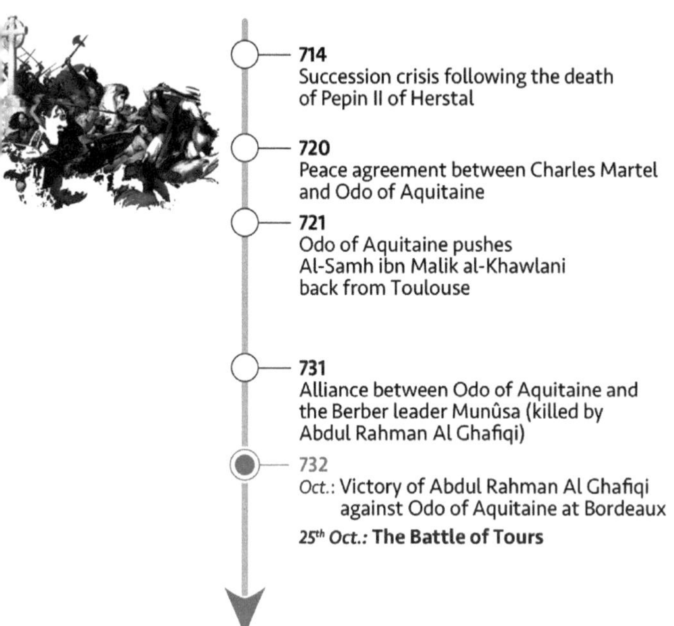

714
Succession crisis following the death
of Pepin II of Herstal

720
Peace agreement between Charles Martel
and Odo of Aquitaine

721
Odo of Aquitaine pushes
Al-Samh ibn Malik al-Khawlani
back from Toulouse

731
Alliance between Odo of Aquitaine and
the Berber leader Munûsa (killed by
Abdul Rahman Al Ghafiqi)

732
Oct.: Victory of Abdul Rahman Al Ghafiqi
against Odo of Aquitaine at Bordeaux

25ᵗʰ Oct.: **The Battle of Tours**

- During the year 710, the territory of Al-Andalus was conquered by the Umayyad troops.
- In 714, the death of Pepin II of Herstal generated a large succession crisis. His illegitimate son Charles, who later became Charles Martel, tried to impose himself.
- The years of 716-719 were marked by numerous battles (Amel, Vinchy, Nery) during which Charles managed to win against the Neustrian mayor of the palace Ragenfred, who was then in alliance with the Duke of Aquitaine, Odo.

- Gradually, several cities of Septimania gave way in the face of the Umayyad incursions – with the exception of Toulouse, where the Duke of Aquitaine Odo repelled the onslaught of the governor of Cordoba, Abdul Rahman Al Ghafiqi, in 721.
- Between 720 and 721, Odo had no choice but to make peace with his opponent, Charles.
- Ten years later, Odo the Great allied with the Berber chief of Cerdanya Munûsa. Therefore, Charles considered their pact of 720-721 to be broken and he decided to subjugate Aquitaine. A punitive expedition against Munûsa was also launched by the men of Wali Abdul Rahman Al Ghafiqi. The latter, calling for a holy war from Pamplona, crossed the Pyrenees with 20 000 men and launched a new wave of incursions in Gaul.
- In 732, Aquitaine was looted and the Arab troops headed back towards the north, with the aim of rallying St. Martin of Tours. Helpless, Odo the Great called on Charles for help.
- On 25 October, the fight between the Franks and the troops of Abdul Rahman Al Ghafiqi took place between Poitiers and Chatellerault. The Aquitanians took the Arab troops and the Wali died on the battlefield. The following day, the Franks found the enemy camp deserted.
- A Frankish defensive riposte to the raid orchestrated by the Umayyad troops, the Battle of Tours sanctified the affirmation of the supremacy of the future Frankish Carolingians against other powers. A real setback for the Arab troops, it symbolized the decline of an empire that, within a century, had come to dominate the whole of the Mediterranean. Although it has been elevated to myth,

the confrontation of 732 still remains a historical symbol and the subject of much controversy.

We want to hear from you!
Leave a comment on your online library
and share your favourite books on social media!

FIND OUT MORE

BIBLIOGRAPHY

- Anon. (1885) *Chronique rimée des derniers rois de Tolède et de la conquête d'Espagne par les Arabes*. Paris: E. Leroux.
- Balard, M., Genet, J.P. and Rouche, M. (1990) *Le Moyen Âge en Occident*. Paris: Armand Colin.
- Carpentier, E. (2000) *Les batailles de Poitiers. Charles Martel et les Arabes*. France: Geste Éditions.
- Gauvard, C., De Libera, A. and Zink, M. (2000) *Dictionnaire du Moyen Âge*. Paris: Presses Universitaires de France.
- Géal, F. (2006) *Regards sur al-Andalus. viiie-xve siècle*. Paris: Éditions Rue d'Ulm.
- Gerbet, M.-C. (1992) *L'Espagne au Moyen Âge. viiie-xve siècle*. Paris: Armand Colin.
- Guichard, P. (2011) *Al-Andalus. 711-1492. Une histoire de l'Espagne musulmane*. Paris: Fayard.
- Lebecq, S. (1990) *Nouvelle histoire de la France médiévale. Les origines franques (Ve-IXe siècles)*. Paris: Seuil.
- Levillain, L. and Samaran, C. (1938) Sur le lieu et la date de la bataille dite de Poitiers de 732. *Bibliothèque de l'école des Chartes*, 99(1), pp. 243-267.
- Michaud, F. and Sénac, P. (2006) La Bataille de Poitiers, de la réalité au mythe. In Arkoun, M. (ed.) *Histoire de l'islam et des musulmans en France du Moyen Âge à nos jours*. Paris: Albin Michel.
- Pirenne, H. (2003) *Mohammed and Charlemagne*. New York: Dover Publications Inc.

- Rouche, M. (1979) *L'Aquitaine des Wisigoths aux Arabes, 418-781. Naissance d'une région.* Paris: Éditions Touzot.
- Rouche, M. (1990) *Le Moyen Âge en Occident.* Paris: Armand Colin.
- Rucquoi, A. (1993) *Histoire médiévale de la Péninsule ibérique.* Paris: Seuil.
- Sénac, P. (2011) *Le Monde musulman : des origines au Xe siècle.* Paris: Armand Colin.
- Tolan, J., Veinstein, G. and Laurens, H. (2012) *Europe and the Islamic World: A History.* New Jersey: Princeton University Press.
- Touati, F.-O. (2000) *Vocabulaire historique du Moyen Âge (Occident, Byzance, Islam).* Paris: La Boutique de l'Histoire Éditions.

ICONOGRAPHIC SOURCES

- *Battle of Tours, October 732* by Charles de Steuben, between 1834 and 1837. Royalty-free reproduction picture.
- *Visigoth King Roderic during the Battle of Gadelate* by Bernardo Blanco y Pérez, 1871. Royalty-free reproduction picture.
- *Pepin the Younger, King of France*, engraving from *Chroniques des ducs de Brabant* by Adrian de Barlande, published in 1603. Royalty-free reproduction picture.
- *St. Boniface Baptizing and Martyrdom in 754*, illustration from the Fulda Sacramentary, fol. 126, 11th century. Royalty-free reproduction picture.
- *Charles Martel, duc de Brabant*, engraving from *Chroniques des ducs de Brabant* by Adrian de Barlande,

published in 1603. Royalty-free reproduction picture.

MUSEUMS

- Museum of Moussais-la-Bataille (France).

IMPROVE YOUR GENERAL KNOWLEDGE

IN A BLINK OF AN EYE !

www.50minutes.com

www.50minutes.com

Ebook EAN: 9782806273123

Paperback EAN: 9782806273130

Legal Deposit: D/2015/12603/646

Cover: © Primento

Digital conception by Primento, the digital partner of publishers.